Resistance, Rebellion, Life

Resistance, Rebellion, Life

·

50 POEMS NOW

·

Edited and introduced by Amit Majmudar

ALFRED A. KNOPF · NEW YORK · 2017

This Is a Borzoi Book Published by Alfred A. Knopf

Copyright © 2017 by Alfred A. Knopf
Introduction copyright © 2017 by Amit Majmudar

All rights reserved. Published in the United States by Alfred A. Knopf,
a division of Penguin Random House LLC, New York,
and in Canada by Random House of Canada, a division of
Penguin Random House Canada Limited, Toronto.

www.aaknopf.com

Knopf, Borzoi Books, and the colophon are registered trademarks of
Penguin Random House LLC.

LCCN: 2017937107
ISBN: 978-1-524-71132-0 (trade paperback) / 978-0-525-52021-4 (ebook)

Cover design by Carol Devine Carson
Book design by Iris Weinstein

Manufactured in the United States of America
First Edition

What is truth?

—PONTIUS PILATE

CONTENTS

breitbart.com. What are they seeing? Keats's definition of truth never sounded dangerous to me until now.

What is truth?

3

I must confess to having disliked political poetry and "protest" poetry for much of my reading life. I felt I knew, beforehand, what the strategies would be, even in the most sophisticated poems. The Human Anecdote. A little gratuitous fragmentation. An ironized incorporation of political language.

I could guess even more reliably what the correct and acceptable political position would be—pacifist, internationalist as opposed to nationalist, and generally left-leaning (more on that in a moment). While I usually sympathize with that outlook, I didn't particularly care to get it in verse. I got plenty of it in the editorial pages of this or that newspaper. Besides, a poem was more likely to simplify the situation than render it more complex. The word "relevant" to describe a poet's work was a red flag for me. I admit, I perpetrated a political poem here or there myself over the years, but I always felt a little dirty afterward, and cleansed my palate with some thoroughly irrelevant mystical or mythical stuff.

Needless to say, I have come a long way. My former attitude was the luxury of a sheltered child who got to his twenties without ever doubting the stability (and, smugly, I know, the superiority) of his country, without disaster. As it did to so many of my generation, 9/11 broke a stupor that should have broken well before. It seems impossible to me that people who weren't alive then will soon be getting their driver's licenses. When I zoom out, much of this country's history since that day seems a fitful, graceless descent to overseas violence and domestic paranoia. Terrorism works.

With my increased awareness of political life came an increased awareness of political poetry. The frank glory of this branch of poetry came into focus, like a Magic Eye stereogram. How much of what was best in poetry was utterly, unabashedly, of its time! You could not understand Milton's relationship to his Satan, that opponent of the King of Kings, without understanding Milton's relationship to Cromwell. The Milton I revered as a reworker of Genesis was also the Milton who authored *Areopagitica*. The anti-Florence rants in Dante that used to make my eyes glaze over got me sitting up and paying attention. Of course, I thought, it was the same for him, this lovehatred of country, this estrangement from half of it. We are always playing Guelphs and Ghibellines. It's just the names and places that change. Yeats, Neruda, Ginsberg: These were the obvious go-to poets for political engagement. I could see the ruptures that an aroused political consciousness seemed to precipitate in the oeuvres of W. S. Merwin and, especially, Adrienne Rich—that transition from filigree to in-your-face.

Politics soaked into every poet, somehow or another—like the trace of atmospheric carbon in a tree ring, indicating a volcanic explosion in a given year. I began discovering the political in places where I least expected it. Censorship worked on genius like a formal restraint, prompting ever greater creativity. Even Shakespeare's sonnets had their "bare ruin'd choirs" that sang, indirectly, of Queen Elizabeth's breaking of Catholic churches.

I have since realized that it's pointless to like or dislike an entire body of poetry. We should judge political poetry in general the same way we would judge a specific anthology of it, by focusing on what is best in it. Plenty of excellent political poetry is being written today—more, as I have learned through my selection process, than can fit between the covers of a book.

4

The young Iosif Dzhugashvili was a fairly successful poet in Georgian. In his teens, his pseudonym was "Soselo." He took the name "Joseph Stalin" only later.

Stalin disowned and suppressed Soselo's poems, but anthologists, even after Stalin's death, kept including the poems on their own merit, attributing them to "Anonymous." Maybe because he had been a poet once, Stalin took an intense and personal interest in the doings of poets. Boris Pasternak once had to field a phone call in which Stalin asked him what to do about Mandelstam.

This is hard for a contemporary American poet to imagine. Today no poet, no matter what kind of pose he or she may strike, is "dangerous" enough to persecute. The worst you get is a little delay in the TSA line, usually prompted, as I can attest, by extrapoetic factors. No poet attracts any malignant interest from the halls of power, at least not yet. In the old totalitarianisms, oddly enough, the bastards actually gave a damn about poetry. You could speak truth to power by writing it because power worried about your quatrains. How can a poet write truth to power when power doesn't read poems?

5

The Internet, proliferating outlets for speech equally free with truth and falsehood, has democratized every source and sequence of words. It has been a mixed blessing: Yes, the old hierarchies have been challenged and undermined, but it has also leveled the poets and liars. The screen equalizes the poem and the fake news story. This began all the way back with Gutenberg. Pamphlets about the royal family, scurrilous or fawning, proliferated in advance of the French Revolution; newspapers proliferated in Russia in the run-up to October 1917, from both the far left and the far right. Today we are witnessing something quite old, only in digital form, and dialed way up.

The freedom to choose your own authority seems to have ended up destroying authority itself. What is truth? The old persecutions of heresy by totalizing monotheisms make a little more sense now. The present moment—with multiple authorities, and the subsequent multiplication of realities—is the situation churchmen and mullahs have dreaded for centuries. Totalizing secular ideologies, too, have persecuted their dissidents as existential threats, whether in Stalinist show trials or McCarthy-era hearings. Our society has taken many simultaneous routes to this one endpoint.

But is it really an endpoint?

Enter the marchers. Enter the leakers. Enter the activists. Enter the truth-tellers.

Enter the fifty poets in this book.

6

How did I end up in such illustrious company? My trail here leads back to the *New York Times* columnist Nicholas Kristof, who ran a contest for political poetry earlier this year. I wrote a sestina that was one of the winners. Its publication led to a conversation with my publisher about the possibility of this anthology.

The sestina, incidentally, was called "Swearing the Oath." The word "oath" pointed both to the citizenship oath and to the archaic sense of "swearing oaths"—the poem concerned, after all, the effects of a backward-looking vulgarian on our society.

Naturalized
In 2016,
My mom watched
Natural-born citizens
Show her the nature
Of America.

"This is not America,"
I said, "this nation of lies!
This is a monster of nature
Spending 2016
Making monsters of citizens!"
She and I watched

Together till I couldn't watch.
So this was America.
So these were her citizens.

How strange, to be naturalized
In 2016,
The year our nature

Warred with our other nature,
And all we could do was watch
Reality show us in 2016
An unreal America.
My mom never felt more unnaturalized
Than in the year she became a citizen.

Good thing she became a citizen
What with a monster of nature's
Narrow unnatural eyes
Impossible not to watch
Leveled, mesmeric, at America
In the year of our lord 2016.

In the year of our liar 2016
My mom became a citizen
Of a strange America.
Improbability, too, is a force of nature.
We couldn't not watch.
Unnatural untruths became natural lies.

In 2016, my mom became a naturalized
Citizen just in time to watch
America denature.

In reality (the one outside the "reality" of the poem), my
mother became a naturalized citizen twenty years ago. So the

poem actually pivots on the "alternative fact" of her swearing the oath in 2016. In a sense, I ended up in charge of this anthology by peddling a fake story in a national newspaper.

What did you expect? All poets are liars.

7

I invited contributors to *Resistance* to write poems of any political leaning, including ones in support of the current president and/or his policies. The far right, after all, casts itself as a resistance and a rebellion, too—against political correctness, globalization, "the elites," and recent demographic and cultural changes. I did not filter the poems that got into this anthology on the basis of ideology.

Though it certainly does *look* like I did. Just like the *Times* contest, which attracted thousands of entries but zero pro-Trump poems, Knopf's call for poems fielded zero pro-Trump poems. Why is this? Why do poets so consistently lean left in our country? I can count the number of truly conservative poets I know on the fingers of one hand. Perspectives vary a great deal in the other professional culture I know, medicine. I usually can't guess how a fellow physician voted. In poetry, it goes without saying.

There are proximal historical factors, of course: The counterculture of the sixties gave rise to a campus culture today that skews left, especially in the humanities and social sciences. Many of our best poets are professors and end up in university towns. The culture of literary awards and festivals tends to foster a guildlike unity of political thought (though not, I should point out, of poetic practice). Historically, artistic cliques and "schools" have formed in big cities. The blue–red color scheme of the electoral map—especially in states like mine, Ohio—matches the urban–rural divide. Talent, whether in the arts and sciences or in business, tends to cluster in geographically small areas; banking, tech, and creative writing benefit from porous borders. They develop their own cultures, their own group-think, their own power centers—Manhattan, Silicon Valley, Iowa.

But there are also deeper, psychological reasons why writerly revulsion is so widespread against Donald Trump specifically. The question "What is truth?," however it's inflected, is get-ting, from hundreds of outraged American writers, the same answer: *Not this.*

We poets are the absolute antitheses of Trump. We are at the other end of the spectrum; we are his negative images. He spits out every coarse thing that crosses his mind, as it occurs to him; we agonize over and refine each phrase we put out there, wondering if it rings true and serves the truth. He wants "heavy vetting" for refugees; we vet our words. He obliterates fine distinctions; we focus on nuances and strive to bring them out. We introspect to expand our empathy, and we strive to communicate that introspective empathy to strangers unlike us; even a writer's self-regard is in the service of the other. He is a narcissist. Many of us seek out voices from other cultures and books translated from foreign languages; he doesn't read. Our audiences are small, and we deserve a larger one; his are far, far larger than he deserves. He lies.

We speak the truth.

8

About fake stories.

Every writer is also a reader, and readerly instinct knows truth on sight. The resistance against the current administration is only secondarily against specific policies. The primary resistance and rebellion—and *revulsion*—has been prompted by a fake story about America and about the world.

We all know the story well enough. The gorge rises at it. The "Judaeo-Christian West" (Jews and Christians even a hundred years ago would have scoffed at this construct) is at war with a monolithic "Islam" (in actuality the most fractious, and starkly fractured, religious community in the world). More stories: "Illegals" are nefarious invaders destroying this country—as opposed to providing, to our collective shame, an exploitable underclass for business owners and private citizens throughout the American Southwest. Or this one: Women are to be valued based on their bodies alone, and graded on a numerical scale.

Some of these false stories originate on the far right, others in the most vulgar sewers of the culture. None of them are particularly new. All of them are repulsive to the kind of people who are creating the best poetry of our time. Many such poets, young and old, are to be found in this slim book. They are poets and believe in the transcendent nature of their art—but they have taken a side. It is the side of resistance, rebellion, and the life of this country.

9

Everyone ends up picking a side. Those fake stories about America and Americans strike millions of our countrymen as instinctively true, just as they strike the poets in this volume as instinctively false. If we are being honest with ourselves, we cannot "know" if we have taken the right side at this moment.

It comes down to belief. What story about yourself, your country, and your people, about our past, present, and future, do you believe in? In which America—in *whose* America—do you place your faith?

The political quarrel of our day has boiled down to a duel of realities. Maybe it was always this way. Maybe all wars are wars of religion. Even when they don't escalate into group violence, though, all wars are wars of words.

And that is what gives me hope. It means that poets still have a role. So do journalists—at least the ones who privilege truth over eyeballs, or try to attract eyeballs with truth. So do placard-scrawlers and people writing letters to their representatives and people who never speak in public giving speeches at a march in front of tens of thousands of strangers. What we are fighting is a false story, or a story we believe to be false.

We have seen false stories before. Whether it's the false story of whites being better than nonwhites, or Aryans being better than Jews and Slavs, or believers being better than infidels, or men being better than women, false stories take a lot of killing because they are made of language. Because they are made of language, though, they can be killed. Or at least beaten back, out of public life.

And so I pass you along to the poets in this volume—warriors, every one, welcoming you to the fight.

10

My own contribution to this anthology, the fiftieth poem, is a cento consisting of at least one line or phrase from the forty-nine poems preceding it. I calculated that the cento, by its very nature, would be in-formed by the heterogeneity of this anthology's contributors—and, by analogy, of our society's members.

My sole original contribution is the final line.

America   America   America

Much like Pilate's question, that line can mean a variety of things, depending on how you inflect and punctuate it. It can be cried in frustration, muttered in disappointment, or declaimed in hope. Or whispered with regret. Or shouted as a question, like the name of a loved one lying on the ground.

How you hear it in your head I leave to you.

—AMIT MAJMUDAR · *Dublin, Ohio*

Resistance, Rebellion, Life

LET THEM NOT SAY *Jane Hirshfield*

Let them not say: we did not see it.
We saw.

Let them not say: we did not hear it.
We heard.

Let them not say: they did not taste it.
We ate, we trembled.

Let them not say: it was not spoken, not written.
We spoke,
we witnessed with voices and hands.

Let them not say: they did nothing.
We did not-enough.

Let them say, as they must say something:

A kerosene beauty.
It burned.

Let them say we warmed ourselves by it,
read by its light, praised,
and it burned.

DARK MATTER ODE   *Rowan Ricardo Phillips*

You'll say you can't remember, you were too
Young, that the idea wasn't yours. Or, maybe
You'll feel the need to feel misunderstood
And say You don't understand, You don't
Understand, You don't. But I was there
When the sky closed. I know that brief darkness
Feels good. That God works on no sleep as certain
As Bre'er Sleep reclining in your lampshade,
Sweet Bre'er Sleep who never knows sleep. His song
Swells in my wrists as they hang on your crib.
Leaning in, inspecting you like a crook,
I am the poet in his pillory.
I see you as free. I sing of the wood.
And I sing of the bars. I am the dunce
Of the stars who sings of the bars.
Poets know time is a dead man walking:
We are all the terrorist Tichborne—.
I love that you sleep so softly despite
The virus of my verbal flailings flowing
Through your veins. One day you will be facing
It, the reflective black immensity
Of it all, and you will seethe and set out
Into a world of science and anger
That I just can't imagine. Today won't
Matter to you because today to you
Won't be by then today, which went like this:
There was the IMAX movie about Dark

Matter and the protests about how Black
Lives matter, but then for you the same sleep
And then a million years from now somewhere
Discovering that something like this one
Moment could have happened, could have mattered,
That you asleep in your crib were a god
In the machine and that poem your father
Wrote you was a fucking living weapon.

RIDDLE

Jericho Brown

We do not recognize the body
Of Emmett Till. We do not know
The boy's name nor the sound
Of his mother wailing. We have
Never heard a mother wailing.
We do not know the history
Of ourselves in this nation. We
Do not know the history of our-
Selves on this planet because
We do not have to know what
We believe we own. We believe
We own your bodies but have no
Use for your tears. We destroy
The body that refuses use. We use
Maps we did not draw. We see
A sea so cross it. We see a moon
So land there. We love land so
Long as we can take it. Shhh. We
Can't take that sound. What is
A mother wailing? We do not
Recognize music until we can
Sell it. We sell what cannot be
Bought. We buy silence. Let us
Help you. How much does it cost
To hold your breath underwater?
Wait. Wait. What are we? What?
What? What on Earth are we?

MOUNTEBANK

David Breskin

Charlatan, huckster, grifter,
fraud: the riches of English
teem with phony gold: sham, quack,
fake, cheat, con. But one term rules,
king for our malevolent
escalator descender
who firmly mounts the public
bench as a loyal German
shepherd mounts a quivering mutt:
by instinct, without a care,
and with a glint in his eye.

CHILDREN OF THE SUN   *Richie Hofmann*

Our minds were minds of many changes.
Our schools were abandoned castles.
The bus driver spoke no German and no English.
His name was Omar and his hair was black.
The street we lived on was called something different then.
In the universities, we chattered in the medieval language
and wrote treatises in the language of modernity.
We knelt in the grass and kissed another boy's wrists.
Tulips grew erect in the tended-to expanse.
We watched documentaries about mass incarceration in
    independent theaters.
We ate spicy soup with ceramic spoons.
A congresswoman was shot, the radio said.
We sat in the car together.
Some people's parents read the newspapers
but most watched TV.
The Jews' paintings circulated in the great museums.
We left our cloth napkins on the table when we exited the
    more fashionable taverns.
We used our phones to send illicit pictures to men we'd never
    meet
and felt turned-on and anonymous.
We felt genuine happiness when our baby sisters were born.
Police walked muzzled dogs through the airports.
We used our phones to read articles about rising anti-
    Semitism in France.

Like other children, we lived between the wars
and felt doomed and lucky.
We lived in New Jersey and Boston, Atlanta, Baltimore, and
    Chicago.
There was violence, and it did and didn't touch us.

JUBILATE HOMO   *Ellen Bass*

After Christopher Smart

For I will consider the transgendered person.

For he or she may be the servant of a less violent world.

For at the first touch of his nipples, he feels breasts roosting
    like plump birds.

For this is done by wreathing his body seven times round with
    elegant longing.

For secondly, he stains his lips—Fire and Ice, Bruised Plum,
    Lasting Kiss.

For thirdly, he who is becoming she cuts the glans into a
    clitoral diamond.

For fourthly, she who is becoming who she always has been
    reverses the phallus to a cave of consolation.

For fifthly, she bleeds.

For sixthly, she lies still with a smooth stent in her vagina.

For seventhly, she carries home groceries in the twilight.

For eighthly, she sleeps hard.

For there is nothing sweeter than her peace when at rest.

For there is little more fierce than the need to be known.

For Artemis cut the soft flesh from her chest, the truer to
    shoot her arrow.

For Joan of Arc cropped her hair and dressed in armor,
    though it meant death.

For jazz musician Billy Tipton married and raised three
    children who discovered his past at his death.

For a wife might not question caresses clothed in darkness,
    if her husband's hands make her feel royal.
For even *he* and *she* are false.
For *it* is tinged with the taste of metal.
For words are struggling to be born like any animal.
For Tiresias could understand birdsong and read the future
    in fire.
For my task is to praise all I don't understand.
For there are more sexes than wildflowers.
For the eye of the male and the eye of the female is the same
    eye, the same dark well of the pupil.
For Passion Star in a Texas jail, let her be safe from those who
    have torn the bud of her anus and razored her face.
For Fred Martinez, Navajo transgender girl, whose killer
    crushed her skull,
whose killer sliced her open at the belly,
whose killer left her dying by the side of the road,
let her be remembered.
For we are delivered to this small earth spinning.
For we are delivered glazed with vernix and blood.
For the truest drum is desire.
For we can divine but a glimpse of what is.
For the streets of our bodies wind as a labyrinth.
For we have only one another to cling to.
To be kind to, to despise.

THEY CALL THEM BLUE MY MIND   *Erica Dawson*

After learning it's fine for some select
people to say *grab them by the pussy,* I,
with my rights and privileges, there,   undo and elect
to sew my labia closed, using a butterfly

loop and Pantone's Black 7 thread. It's then
I'm most colored.
                    Bleeding.
                              Now the man who said,
You're black even down there, girl, says, *Say when,
woman,* and I tell him I've never bled

the bright red of a finch but, often, I
assume the brown body of a cactus wren—

ass up, chest out, and strength enough to fly
through a closed door, just bust inside where ten

evolvulus, bluer than bruises, hit
with no sunlight, refuse to wilt, and will
their way through thirsty—thin bodies unfit
for death like a bleeding woman standing, still.

MARBLES AND A DEAD BEE   *D. Nurkse*

Def. Noun. 1. The final and fully developed adult
stage of an insect . . . 2. An unconscious idealized
mental image of someone, especially a parent . . .

—OXFORD DICTIONARIES

1

Imago was elected this morning—
in the gray hour before dawn
the last firewall crumbled.
A street drunk moans
in ecstasy or shame.

2

Close your eyes. Imago controls
the House, Senate, Supreme Court.
Open them. Just sunlight on a blind.

3

As a dropped bulb shatters
so my country.

4

The poet will defend herself with poetry,
the lover with sex,
the child with marbles and a dead bee,
the suicide with suicide.

5

But if you choose to kill yourself
find a quiet room in the past.

Tonight your life is required for a task.

THE MOON AFTER ELECTION DAY   *Alex Dimitrov*

I'm looking at the moon tonight,
the closest it's been to Earth since 1948
and feel relieved we can do little to ruin it.
That can't be true, you say, and for a moment
even the moon's loneliness escapes isolation
and depends on something else. It's attached.
Like us and what we abandon. Us
and the evil we refuse. The same evil
we share history with, the thin membrane
between you or me and the worst of life.
It's already past midnight and another election
is over in the United States of America.
The oceans will not continue into infinity.
Nor will our money. Nor will this suffering.
We have voted and proven again
we do not know one another. *I am trying
so hard to understand this country,* I tell you
even as I'm about to fail loving you (I know this)
in the way people need to be loved
which is without deception, which is almost
impossible. *Don't you love it though,* you say,
and I remember the first time I saw you in a room
without anyone else. *Don't you love the moon?*
And because it's easy to say it, I do, I make sure
to tell you *I do.* Despite the news I knew years ago:
no one saves anyone. We're on the moon.

THE ELEPHANT IN THE ROOM   *Kay Ryan*

The room is
almost all
elephant.
Almost none
of it isn't.
Pretty much
solid elephant.
So there's no
room to talk
about it.

CIVICS ONE: OUR DEMOCRACY   *Richard Kenney*

As kids we're taught it's safe as pyramids,
unshakable and permanent amidst
a sordid history amok with ids

frocked in all those lesser *ocracies*
the mind of man has proffered up, all crazy,
and all doomed to end up like the auk.

(Plus, it's *Athenian,* we think. Pax Plato;
smart man, but no one bats a thousand). Later,
though, we see it's really safe as plates

awhirl on broomsticks. Trump! And now we're all
ears, waiting for the fools with whom we've quarreled
to aggregate a mob for all the world

like all the mobs in storybooks: the slaking
rage that spatters from the joke when Loki
rules the moot: *we thought it was OK.*

*Thought nothing could go really wrong. We thought
the fire we played with wasn't all that hot.
We thought we could control it, and could not.*

KILLING METHODS   *Ada Limón*

Outside, after grieving for days,
I'm thinking of how we make stories,
pluck them like beetles out of the air,

collect them, pin their glossy backs
to the board like the rows of stolen
beauties, dead, displayed at Isla Negra,

where the waves broke over us
and I still loved the country, wanted
to suck the bones of the buried.

Now I'm outside a normal house
while friends cook and please
and pour secrets into each other.

A crow pierces the sky, ominous,
clanging like an alarm, but there
is no ocean here, just tap water

rising in the sink, a sadness clean
of history only because it's new,
a few weeks old, our national wound.

I don't know how to hold this truth,
so I kill it, pin its terrible wings down
in case, later, no one believes me.

DAILY APOCALYPSE

Dean Young

Saw a door on a truck going by
swing open.
Saw a guy in an acid-yellow
vest inspecting the corner
green puddle that never evaporates
wave as in waving me in.
A mocking bird concurred
with a car alarm. Someone
had dropped a purple spaceman in.
Aphrodite rose from the mist
as crazily as flowers eat meat.
Tried to go to a museum
but ended up in a weapons depot,
everyone stunned like there's a hole
in their chest and they're struggling
through peacock guts. Is Beatlemania
at last dead? How about English Departments?
The soul is iron. Plunge it from fire
into ice, it shines. One of these days,
I'll refuse to fill out the green form
just to get the blue form as if
everything isn't already permanently
seething formlessness and meat-eating flowers.
I'm just like you.
I wasn't made by their god.
My vote never counts.

"YOU WILL NEVER GET DEATH / OUT OF YOUR SYSTEM"

Dana Levin

November 12, 2016. Day 4.

—

How old is the earth? I asked my machine, and it said: Five great extinctions, one in process, four and a half billion years.

It has always been very busy on Earth: so much coming and going! The terror and the hope ribboning through that.

Death, like a stray dog you kick out of the yard who keeps coming back—its scent of freedom and ruin—

> Some people love death so much they want to give it to everyone.
>
> Some are more selective.
>
> Some people don't know they're alive.

—

Metabolic system, financial system, political system, eco-system—systems management, running around trying to put out fires—

Sodium nitrate. Sodium benzoate. Butylated Hydroxyanisole
    (to keep the food from rotting). Plastic (surgery). Botox,
    Viagra, cryo-chamber—

Voting backwards, into what
    has already died—

Voting Zombie in the name of "change"—

And everywhere in fortune cookies, the oracular feint of a
    joke future—

where death is the trick candle on the victory cake.

                    —

Some truths are hard to accept. Especially when they won't
    budge beyond a couplet.

Especially when they won't tell you if they mean you well, if
    they herald freedom or ruin—

You! You and Death! Lovers who just can't quit. That's how
    we make the future.

The terror and the hope of that, as change goes viral.

Studies suggest *How may I help you officer?* is the single most disarming thing to say and not *What's the problem?* Studies suggest it's best the help reply *My pleasure* and not *No problem.* Studies suggest it's best not to mention *problem* in front of power even to say there is none. Gloria Steinem says women lose power as they age and yet the loudest voice in my head is my mother. Studies show the mother we have in mind isn't the mother that exists. Mine says: *What the fuck are you crying for?* Studies show the baby monkey will pick the fake monkey with fake fur over the furless wire monkey with milk, without contest. Studies show to negate something is to think it anyway. *I'm not sad.* I'm not sad. Studies recommend regular expressions of gratitude and internal check-ins. Studies define assertiveness as self-respect cut with deference. *Enough,* the wire mother says. History is a kind of study. History says we forgave the executioner. Before we mopped the blood we asked: *Lord Judge, have I executed well?* Studies suggest yes. *What the fuck are you crying for, officer?* the wire mother teaches me to say, while America suggests *Solmaz, have you thanked your executioner today?*

THE VOW

Eileen Myles

Everything's like a shade
of brightness and dark
like this new pad
I got
or my computer
or these doorways opening
one to the next
which is where I
began. Nothing is like
my dog eating an
apple core in bed
The sleeping
bag is read. It's March
and it's already
warm. I don't want
you stepping on
my computer which is
where all my friends
are, some of whom are Nazis
I never thought I'd call Nazis
friends but I spend
at least an hour
a night w these ones &
then I wake up
and read about
the real ones on
Twitter. For days Rebecca

Solnit
& I struggled to be
facebook friends.
It was like we were
going to the gym
together. We worked
it out. I was visiting
her today looking
at her face. The heat
just rumbled. It's not
even evening but I
thought I'd get
a little nazi
in early. I would die
for my country
if that included
everything, my friends,
and my dogs
and all the lakes
and ponds. I
am ready
for the struggle.

LOVE POEM FOR AN APOCALYPSE   *Dave Lucas*

I wish I'd met you after everything had burned,
after the markets crash and global sea levels rise.
The forests scorched. The grasslands trespassed.
My love, it is a whole life's work to disappear—
ask the god with his head in the wolf's mouth or
the serpent intent on swallowing all the earth.
Ask the senate subcommittee for market solutions
for late capitalism and early-onset dementia.
You and a bird flu could make me believe in fate.
I think we might be happy in the end, in the dark
of a hollow tree, a seed bank or blast-proof bunker,
if only you would sing the song I love, you know
the one about our precious eschatology, the one
I always ask to hear to lull me back to sleep.

NEW YEAR

Joanna Klink

We woke to the darkness before our eyes,
unable to take the measure of the loss.
Who are they. What are we. What have we
  abandoned to arrive with such violence at this hour.
In answer we drew back, covered our ears
with our hands to the heedless victory, or vowed,
  as I did, into the changed air, never to consent.
But it was already too late, too late for the unfarmed fields,
the men by the station, the park swings, the parking lots,
  the groundwater, the doves—too late for dusk
falling in summer, chains of glass lakes
  mingled into dawn, the corals, the neighbors,
the first drizzle on an empty street, cafeterias and stockyards,
young men asking twice a day for
  work. Too late for hope. Too far along
to meet a country, a people, its annihilating need.

Because the year is new and the great change
already under way, we concede a thousandfold
  and feel, harder than the land itself,
a complicity for everything we did not see
or comprehend: cynicism borne of raw despair,
long-cultivated hatreds, the promises of leaders
traveling like cool silence through the dark.
My life is here, in this small room, and like you
  I am waiting to know—but there is no time

to wait for what has happened.
What does the future ask of me,
those who won't have enough to eat by evening,
those whose disease will now take hold—
   and the decades that carry past me once I've died,
generations of children, the suffering that is never solved,
the heat over the earth, its marshes,
   its crowded towers, its unbreathable night air.
I would open my hand from the wrist,
step outside, not lose nerve.
Here is the day, still to be lived.
We do not fully know what we do.
But the trains depart the stations, traffic lurches
   and stalls, a highway crew has paused.
Desert sun softens the first color of the rock.
Who governs now governs by grievance and old scores,
   but we compass our worth,
prepare to do the work not our own,
and feel, past the scorn in his eyes, the burden
in the torso of a stranger, draw close to the sick,
   the weak, the women without jobs, the twelve-year-old
facing spite half-tangled into sleep, the panic
tightening inside everyone who has been told to go,
I will help you although I do not know you,
and strive not to look away, be unwilling to profit,
   an ache inside that endless effort,
a slowed-down summons not from those

whose rage is lit by greed—we *do not consent*—
but the ones who wake without prospect,
those who don't speak, cannot recover,
   like the old woman at the counter, the helpless father
who, like you, gets no more than his one life.

From SOFT TARGETS   *Deborah Landau*

There were real officers in the street,
but they were doing it wrong.

One winked at me. Another was purely conceptual.
One thought to himself as I walked by
you little bitch.

Bulge-knobs of their guns
made them aural made them real big machismo,
even the skinny ones, even the abstract.

A certain beauty in the duty of it
the absence of pleasantries, cold and uniformed.

Meanwhile he was broken, she was concussed
and we returned home, gilded with what, safety?

In advance of danger animals agitate.

When the time comes all this
will be only shouts and disturbance.

Now bring me a souvenir from the desecrated city.
Something tender, something that might bloom.

WE'VE COME A LONG WAY
TOWARD GETTING NOWHERE

Bob Hicok

My obsession with Jews is an obsession
with one Jew. I look at her walking
and wonder what anyone could have
against Jews, at her sleeping
or hunting for her keys in the morning,
which she does often, lose her keys
when she has to go to work, suggesting
she doesn't want to, and maybe this
is the problem with Jews:
they don't want to leave. Or they eat
lots of chicken. Or worry the black
of their skirts doesn't match the black
of their tops. Or like children more
than babies. Or fret over their mothers.
My Jewish problem is figuring out
why America in 2016 has a dab
of 1930s German Fascism to it—
people at political rallies
yelling crap about the Jews.
If I thought it would do any good,
I'd go to Topeka or wherever
and bring Eve with her troubled wardrobe
and her love of chicken and fascination
with children between two and thirteen,
when they can talk but before
they've begun planning the murder

of their parents, bring her face-to-face
with the screamers and ask, So these
are the freckles you hate? I would—we have
a lot of Amex points and I've never been
to Topeka or wherever, and I'm sure wherever
is very nice. And whenever we travel
to wherever, whatever people say
and however they say it, Eve's freckles
will be the same, kind of cute
and kind of Jewish,
just like all her other parts
that do and do not have freckles,
in an inventory I alone
get to take, though trust me—
after repeated inspection, I can attest
that underneath it all, she, like many
of the people you know or are,
is ticklish, wrinkly, sexy, scarred—
since Jews really are relentless
when it comes to being human.

FACING THE END   *David St. John*

I wake up in the morning and I wonder
Why everything's the same as it was
I can't understand, no, I can't understand
How life goes on the way it does

—SKEETER DAVIS, "The End of the World"

I joined my friends as we dove face-first into a blazing rage
    & we started seeing one another

On the streets again not the hallowed auditoriums of
    commerce all of us trying to jump-start our way

Out of despair so I simply embraced my full-frontal nostalgia
    for everything from the 60s

Most of all the marches & tear gas & being tossed crumpled
    as cartoons by water cannons

Those blind naked days of being just 18 & filled with the
    clarity of wild injustice & the way money hates people

& when she marched in the Capitol Anna's sign was of
    American Gothic but she'd given Mother

A Klan hood & Father an orange ball cap & she'd presciently
    pasted above his head the bare gilt

Cupola of the Ivan the Great Bell Tower in the Kremlin
   complex & as I stood back watching other marchers

Stop her to photograph that sign with the Washington
   Monument erect & white behind her

I turned & looked to see the end of the mile-plus of knit
   kitties—but there was no end anyone could see

& in a moment it came back to me that scent of wet
   barricades & the old actual once lost

Now again familiar first fresh taste of radical human liberty

IMMIGRATION ANTHEM   *Sharon Olds*

I bring you a tired song of my poor
femur-knob, aching before
the hip-op. I huddled this morning under
the covers—the leg weighs twice as much as the
other leg by now, I swing its
masses of fluid along like an enclosed
falls. My mother told me that her people
had come here from across the sea,
yearning to sing to their God of crags
and thistles, to breathe free, men and
women who made war naked, painted
blue, attacked by their landlords who saw them
as wretched refuse—garbage, teeming
with vermin. They had pushed off from that shore and
floated homeless on the ocean, through calm
and tempest—sometimes in sight of a fountain
tossed up out of the brow of one
whose house the water was—until
they came to these islands and low hills
which lift up from a land where we have
set a lamp with a golden torch
on top, to remind us, here at the door:
entering through it was a promise to leave it
open behind us.

THE DEATH OF CAPTAIN AMERICA   *James Arthur*

Cap will be buried in his costume, in his half-mask,
with his bulletproof shield of blue, red, and white,
and the Invincible Iron Man is inconsolable,
now that Captain America is dead.

If the man inside the coffin was a symbol, what ideals
did he represent? Did he believe in the right to bear arms,
or in big government? Was he disfigured from battle?
Did he have a schoolboy's face?
For some, he was an authoritarian endowed with physical
    grace,
but this morning even the paparazzi
seem moved by the manly grief of the mighty Thor.
What will become of the Pax Americana
now that Captain America is dead?

If he stormed the beach at Normandy
was he in the shadows at the hanging of Saddam Hussein?
Cap's enemy the Kingpin is here,
leaning on a diamond-encrusted cane.
Cap never drank, never smoked, was straight
as a bug-collector's pin,
but many a crooked man will walk a crooked mile
now that Captain America is dead.

The escalator's been broken since August.
The drinking fountain is full of cement.

Will the train stations descend into ruin
now that Captain America is dead?

Some people want a moral. Some, only a refrain.
Some want to go on injuring themselves
in the way they have
time and again,
but who will speak for the man inside the coffin—
his love of slapstick, his wide-open grin?
Will anyone speak of the man himself,
remembering what was best and worst in him?

Into the ground, the indestructible shield,
the myth, the one-man legion. Into the ground,
the man, the boy, and every toy or comic book
that ever pleased him. Into the ground.
Into the ground. Into the ground.
Captain America is dead.

BORDER PATROL AGENT   *Eduardo C. Corral*

Summer is a puta. I park
                    beneath branches, crank up the AC
                                        in the Jeep.
I hate the rearview mirror.
    It makes me look like my father. Chaste
                        & singed. Last week,
beneath a sky Walmart blue,
        in a clearing full of bottles, sneakers,
                                    TP rolls,
I found a body. Legs
                gnawed to the knees, barbed wire tight
                                        around
the throat.
            I remembered graffiti
                    on a boulder: *God
is always hungry.*
    Sometimes, with binoculars,
                                    I watch wild horses
hurry through the heat. Once
            a yearling stopped mid-gallop

then collapsed
    into a bed of coals the rain could not extinguish.
                                    The radio
is always crackling:
        *six wets sighted on infrared,
                    need a spic speaker stat . . .*

I only speak Spanish with my father.
                    He often mistakes blue parakeets

                                        perched

on the stove for gas flames.
                    Last July, far from Tucson,
                              I found a rape tree:
torn panties draped on branches.
                    The tree a warning,
                              a way for smugglers
to claim terrain.
    Lightning climbs a hillside like a stilt walker.

                                        Rain

strikes the windshield.
                    I think of my wife
                              asleep on her side. Breasts
pressed together
          as if one were dreaming the other.

                                        Her womb

empty.
    My dick useless.
                    There are things I just can't tell her.
Sometimes only body parts remain.
                              They're buried
in baby caskets.

NEGOTIATIONS   *Michael Dickman*

White people
my brothers & sisters
caucus in their
holes

They would turn over a bus full of schoolkids & set that on
    fire

Have done

I believe in hoop rolling my heart into the sea like a wet
    dream
I believe in Xmas lights from the 50s & fried chicken

Oh let's
give them what
they want: no jobs just

more heroin
more heroin
more heroin

SOME SAY

Some say it's High Noon in a big hat, shooting
up the saloon. America? Some say it's your

Second Amendment, those stockpiles of ammo
bought at a chain. Say the next-door kid living in

screen games: exploding heads, walking dead?
Or it's gangs in torched neighborhoods, drugs

running in the brain or a bead drawn on a clinic
doctor, women in line next to a homeless vet,

begging. Some say it's armed revolt, racist cops,
bragging hunters, looter-tools, mass crave/rave

for oblivion: rapture addicts! Here comes one
more drive-by, school invasion, nightclub terror,

bully/bullied, lynch mob, god cult, toddler-a-cide.
O America, shooting from the hip, from the last of

the trees in a national park, your militia surrounded
by SWAT. Say you're an upstanding patriot in an

invented war—defending unborn lobbyists, a double-
sided coin minted by the National Reprisal Association

of the craven congressionals—saying it to history's
final judge. You, great god Gun, in whom some trust:

in bunker-mind, underground condos. O say it in Homeric
chanted dactyls: I sing of arms & the punk self-pumped-

up lovers of the Silencer. Dickinson wrote it first,
living god of Gun, you are "without the power to die."

INSPECTION

Rebecca Hazelton

First we shuffled off
        our shoes, then emptied
our pockets, each of us depositing
        our wallets and keys
        into plastic trays.

Then we unzipped
        the coats that made us look bigger,
    we removed
        our belts and left them neatly looped.

Cufflinks fell to the ground
        like bullets—we laughed at this,
nervously—the women pulled pins
        from their hair
            and had never looked
            so beautiful.

Our hands trembled
but the shirts came off,
        then we each stood on one leg, the other,
and tugged off our pants,
        we placed our underwear
        into the plastic bags and submitted

to a series of questions
        regarding our intent,

the duration
of our stay.

Each of us still had the fine hairs
                on our arms and legs
                that raise in response
                                to drafts of cool air,
and they did rise,
                they did wave like cilia,
which was telling

                but there was more
                                to discover,
certain falsehoods
we'd made
                about our eyes and teeth,
about our hearts
and microwaves,

                and those of us
                                who'd held
                                our children's hands
were asked politely
                to let go, let go,

                no one, we were told,
                                goes in but alone,
                and then we raised our arms,
                                and we walked through.

NATIONAL PARK   *Fady Joudah*

We saw a lot more of them dead than alive
the living diffident by the side of the road
as the far-off mountains flanked and intoxicated
the speedometer into saunter

The dead were interspersed on the asphalt
their poor vision uncorrected by their auditory keenness
like a blind spot in a poet

and their fender-mangled corpses
were occasionally ripped in two
before vultures reached them

In our rental van
we left no mother bereft
and orphaned no piglets

Turkey buzzards and American vultures
were the javelinas' gift to us

red and black scavengers
that perched on ranchland fences
the full span of highway
they'd circle above in diminishing downward spirals

or flinch at each other's puffs and swells
or away from incoming vehicles

Still they shared the dead among them
as we sometimes share our dead
when we love our dead

Javelina the Arabic word for mountain
in its root and then the mountain
coming closer to an ear
became a spear

WE LIVED HAPPILY
DURING THE WAR   *Ilya Kaminsky*

And when they bombed other people's houses, we

protested
but not enough, we opposed them but not

enough. I was
in my bed, around my bed America

was falling: invisible house by invisible house by invisible
    house.

I took a chair outside and watched the sun.

            In the sixth month
of a disastrous reign in the house of money

in the street of money in the city of money in the country of
    money,
our great country of money, we (forgive us)

lived happily during the war.

THE SOURCE   *Joshua Mehigan*

Water is the least environmentally impactful bev-
erage and bottled water is the most environmen-
tally responsible packaged drink choice.

—INTERNATIONAL BOTTLED
WATER ASSOCIATION

Far from these woods and this river, far from the Source,
in a made place not easy to comprehend,
harder than woods and river but much less hard,
where sky and grass are priceless or must be shared,
and shade is rectilinear and smooth;
where the scourge teems upward in tall elaborate mounds,
and doom seeps outward, settling a dull gray crust
over what once were woods and river like these;
in the back of a double-locked shelter in a room where salt
and bread are kept safe from the rain, from rats and starlings,
in a humming iron chest that holds inside it
fresh weather like that of a day between fall and winter;
on a crowded shelf of that chest stands a vessel pressed
from molecules of degraded plantlife and creatures;
and there, in that thin vessel—that is where
the creature, exiled forever from the Source,
further and further cut off from woods and river,
keeps for itself eight handfuls of the river.
It opens the door of the chest. It stands and drinks.
The once-living bottle is see-through like the contents,
the label of vegetable fiber the color of envy.

GOOD BONES   *Maggie Smith*

Life is short, though I keep this from my children.
Life is short, and I've shortened mine
in a thousand delicious, ill-advised ways,
a thousand deliciously ill-advised ways
I'll keep from my children. The world is at least
fifty percent terrible, and that's a conservative
estimate, though I keep this from my children.
For every bird there is a stone thrown at a bird.
For every loved child, a child broken, bagged,
sunk in a lake. Life is short and the world
is at least half terrible, and for every kind
stranger, there is one who would break you,
though I keep this from my children. I am trying
to sell them the world. Any decent realtor,
walking you through a real shithole, chirps on
about good bones: This place could be beautiful,
right? You could make this place beautiful.

INTERVIEW WITH A
BORDER MACHINE

Juan Felipe Herrera

can you please state your name
        Xochitl Tzompantli
what kind of name is that
            it was given to me by an Indian woman
                black hair long black shawl—it
                    means *Skull Rack Flower*
well let's get to business here   why
are you here in the first place
            i do not
            talk about
            that   all i know
                                        eyes
            swim   before
            me   a river
            eyes
            fall upon   me w/candles
                fire in their blood
            to   come—
what do you tell them
            nothing
why are you speaking to me
            —dying falling   wars
                    everything inside of   me is
                    alive & dying at the
                sametime against each   other
what do you know about war you are nothing

but a wall
              a lie   touch me
              like they
              touch me
              climb upon me
              like they give
              their deepest bones—i
              carry a severed withering
              night unto night
        inside
        you will find   my name
        written on a piece of your flesh
you are a bit dramatic i am just interested in
a simple & short interview
              of course everyone is
              anything else   ?
why are you here besides being a hard-working
border apparatus
                            i give you
                            meaning
come on that is easy
              every one of you
              eats from my flesh as i
              eat from the flesh of those inside
              of me the flesh of hunger travelers
              that press me   sharpen
              inside of   me make me
                            call me from afar
              nail me   pour themselves

into me   take me to the   sky threads
i feed
meaning i
prepare a place   more for you
than for   them
i have no idea what you are saying
it does
not matter
you are a listener
of things
that
is
all
well ok ok what about
your friends plans projects hobbies like that
i do not have such
things as   friends
ok well we are done
wait—
my name is Xochitl Tzompantli
Skull Rack Flower i am
the life-cutter the eater
watchtowers guards artillery
wires & codes & dogs &
filth nourish me
i provide
ghosts unclaimed that tie you to a circle
of tortured faces that on occasion
appears as a rose on your suit

i

      bow down to them i remember them
         i ask them to
             forgive me but
all they see is

            you

112TH CONGRESS BLUES

Tomás Q. Morín

Between those symbols of vision the pyramid
and eagle In God We Trust sits in sturdy
caps where it has testified since the 1955
Congress yoked Yahweh to the sawbuck,
which the nickel would say was about time
because it had been preaching the faith
ever since the last days of Lincoln, though
back then it carried a shield and not
the mug of Jefferson, he of the splendid
mind that cleansed the Gospels of Plato
by that miracle of miracles called reading
until all that was left was a Jefferson Jesus
who was wearing tye-wigs when he ascended
to the dome of Monticello from where
on a day without clouds he could see
down from the little mountain past the apple
and peach trees all the way to the debating
loons on Capitol Hill who believed then and now
in evil, that there is a hell with a devil
two shades redder than Oklahoma
dirt, that you can know him by his goat
hoof, or his less famous chicken foot
which you can buy, nails intact, at the grocery store
where they are called chicken paws, not feet,
which is no doubt for the squeamish
who can't bring themselves to eat a foot,
though they have probably chewed

and ripped apart a fried leg or a breast
with such enthusiasm it would make a hen
or two probably faint at the sight and to
the good vegetarians wondering where
is the divine justice in all of this tearing
of flesh they have only to listen to the crunch
of the special recipe skin as it cuts the cheek
and gums of my brother carnivores
just enough for one of my kind to yell *Goddamn*
and call up his state rep who knowing nothing
better to do proposes a law that already
exists when he should instead order
a two-piece special with a biscuit
and bleed a little, and run his tongue over it
until he can remember for our country
it's never really been about money
or God as about the pain in which we trust.

PLAGUE   *David Yezzi*

Some ancient stories begin with a sickness—
Ilium, Egypt, Thebes. The cause is hidden

from the sufferers, at least for the time being,
though slowly they begin to guess at it.

A mother holds her drowned child in her lap.
A man to remain a man is shot to death.

Abandoned and hell-bent, they flee in droves.
Many turn to magic for protection.

And those who foresee red tides get ignored.
The sands, where bodies lie unburied, scroll

past us, in glowing outposts of attention.
Or on nearby streets. Staggering, the number.

What does their ruler—wittingly or not—
keep from them of the evil that began it:

inhuman wrath and blinding counter-wrath?
And in the stalled line of mid-morning traffic,

each driver views the sky through charcoal glass
and feels just how he has a right to feel.

THE BEAVERS

"They flood the pasture," my neighbor explained
when we met this morning at the property line
that divides his field from mine, which is also

a meadow, although I call it a pasture
when talking to him, since a meadow is not
a place his cows would roam, but a patch

of paradise for picnics and lovers.
We had just been walking around to see
what damage winter had done to the fence

and trees when we met at the marker and greeted
each other, then broached the weather and other
things regarding spring: the sap,

its grade, its run, the snow, the herd, the beavers.
"They're heading this way as we speak,"
he said. "I saw them in a dream last night."

Spirits, I thought, *come back to teach
the mysteries of building houses in water,*
but nodded instead like a dashboard doll.

*Elders in the ruse of beavers with a genius
for damming,* I wanted to tell him,
but couldn't stop nodding in

agreement with his denial of the fun
he has each summer exploding their houses
with TNT, then shooting them

from behind a wall. "Pests," he called
them, when he really meant such perfect
moving targets for catching in the hairs

of his .243. "Good luck,"
I said in a tone he didn't catch
as I continued down the row

of giant maples to the stream
to see if I could find some sign
of them, as I had in previous years—

the prints of little hands in the loam
and eaten trees, but nothing yet,
just the cold dark water of Sacketts

Brook beneath the silence of a cloudless
sky where a red-tailed hawk besieged
by sparrows let out a cry and then another.

From REFUGEE FUGUE   *A. E. Stallings*

I
Aegean Blues

The sea is for holidaymakers, summer on the beach,
Surely there is space enough to spread a towel for each;
Dry land isn't something you should pray to reach.

Look, how glad our kids are, making their sandy town,
And how they build the battlements the laughing waves tear
    down.
But it's the selfsame water where some swim and others
    drown.

The sea is full of dangers, the shallows and the deep.
The sea is full of treasures, down there five fathoms deep,
The sea is full of salt: there are no more tears to weep.

The ferryman says we cross tonight; and everyone pays cash.
Charon don't take Mastercard, you have to pay him cash.
The water seems so calm tonight, you hardly hear the splash.

There was a boy named Icarus; old Daedalus's son.
He turned into a waxwing, black against the sun.
Drowned because he tried to fly. (He's not the only one.)

Why would a kid lie in the sand, and not take off his shoes?
Why would he lie there face down, the color of a bruise?
The sea can make you carefree, nothing left to lose.

There's indigo and turquoise, there's cobalt, sapphire, navy,
And there's a dark like wine, my love, out where things get
    wavy.
Listen, that's the worry note, reminds me of my baby.

IV
APPENDIX A:
USEFUL PHRASES IN ARABIC, FARSI/DARI AND GREEK
(found poem, from the Guide to Volunteering in Athens,
as updated for March 17, 2016)

Welcome to Greece!
Thank God for your safe arrival (greeting after trip)
Hello
Good morning
Good evening
Good night
Thank you
You're welcome
Please
I don't understand
I don't speak Arabic / Farsi

Slowly
Come here
You're safe
Are you wet / cold?
Yes / No
My name is . . .
What is your name?
He / She / It is
We / They are
God is with the patient (will make people laugh)
Give yourself a break (comforting words)
free (no charge)
refugee
volunteer
foreigner
friend
I am hungry
thirsty
food
water
Does it hurt?
sick
pregnant
mother / father
brother / sister
child
family
What country is your family from?
pharmacy

medicine
hospital
doctor
tent
Sorry, it has run out
We do not have it now
New shoes only if yours are broken
Wait here, please
I will return soon
Follow me / come with me
Come back in . . .
5 / 15 / 45 minutes
one hour
quarter / half hour / half day
today / tomorrow / yesterday
How many people?
Sorry
Stay calm
One line, please

Next person

EXILE AND LIGHTNING   *Robert Pinsky*

You choose your ancestors our
Ancestor Ralph Ellison wrote.

Now, fellow-descendants, we endure a
Moment of charismatic indecency
And sanctimonious greed. Falsehood
Beyond shame. Our Polish Grandfather
Milosz and African American Grandmother Brooks
Endured worse than this.
Fight first, then fiddle she wrote.

Our great-grandmother Emma Lazarus
Wrote that the flame of the lamp of the
Mother of Exiles is "Imprisoned lightning."

My fellow children of exile
And lightning, the indecency
Constructs its own statuary.
But our uncle Ernesto Cardenal
Says, *sabemos que el pueblo
la derribará un día.* The people

Will tear it down. Milosz says,
Beautiful and very young, meaning recent,
Are poetry and philo-sophia, meaning science,
Her ally in the service of the good . . .

Their enemies, he wrote, *have delivered*
Themselves to destruction.

"Un dia," and *"very young"*—that long
Ancestral view of time:
Inheritors, *el pueblo,* fellow-exiles:
All the quicker our need to
Fight and make music. As Gwendolyn
Brooks wrote, *To civilize a space.*

SITTING ON A SOFA IN A 1925 BUNGALOW IN ANN ARBOR, MICHIGAN

Cody Walker

On my screen, I see the bronze butterfly,
Awake at the jutting podium,
Blowharding like a thief in green shadow.
Down the ravine behind the empty promises,
The lobbyists follow one another
Into the distances of the afternoon.
To my alt-right,
In a swamp of reproach between two bushes,
The droppings of last year's candidates
Blaze up into golden parachutes.
I lean forward, as the video buffers and comes on.
A chicken hawk floats by, looking for a cabinet post.
I have wasted my life.

THE SOUNDING   *Forrest Gander*

What closes and then
luminous? What opens
and then dark? And into
what do you stumble
but this violet
extinction? With
froth on your lips.
8:16 a.m. The morning's
sleepy face

rolls its million
eyes. Migrating flocks
of your likesame species
incandesce
into transparency.
A birdwatcher lifts

her binoculars. The con-
tinuous with or without
your words
situates you here
(here (here)) even while

you knuckle your eyes
in disbelief. Those

voices you love (human
and not), can you
hear their echoes
hissing away like
an ingot's candescent
scale hammered
on some
blacksmith's anvil?
And behind those
voices, *what is that*
blowing
the valves of your
ears open as black
rain, not in torrents, but
ceaselessly comes
unchecked out of everywhere
with nothing
to slacken it.

THE AMERICAN SECURITY AGAINST
FOREIGN ENEMIES ACT   *Lucie Brock-Broido*

Why do you feel "most vulnerable." Where,
In Damascus, were you born. To whom do you
Pray. What does it mean to have winged
Brows. Have you ever spoken, Ma'am,
Through a mesh. Was it dark speech that you made.
Is it hot inside your burqa. Who
Was Frank Sinatra. Why was our war
Called "Civil" and who won.
Can you keep a bright gaze. How tall
Was Allah. What once was Palestine.
What most displaces you. Have you visited
Somalia. Have you ever crossed a border
In a boat, by night, to another land.
Sir, in all how many died.
Is your wife considered meek.
Point to Mecca from right here.
Why is our court Supreme.
What does the Sound and the Fury
Mean to you. Who was Huckleberry Finn.
Has your husband ever traveled to Afghanistan.
In Sharia, when a woman's hair is loose,
Is she a prostitute or slave.
Do you understand what "Red State" means.
Do you speak American. Here,
Read that aloud.
Do you have tattoos. What does

Paranoia mean. In what season
Do we vote for President. How much freedom
Does the First Amendment cost.
Which is the tallest tree. You were once
A doctor; how is it, as you say, you've
Come to selling vegetables.
How tall was Jesus in bare feet;
Do you consider him a refugee.
Have you a disease that is contagious.
What are "The Hunger Games."
Who sang "Moon River" best.
Do you have friends or relatives
Who are barbarians.
What is the Blues.
What is a Second Sleep. What
Most once made you weep.
When was Lincoln. Who is Stephen King.
Explain what "obfuscation" means.
Have you been lashed.
Who were our pilgrims; why did they come.
Have you ever eaten eel.
Why do you bring just one small son.
Where are the other ones.
What are your other sons.

MONEY ROAD   *Kevin Young*

> *For John T Edge*

On the way to Money,
    Mississippi, we see little
ghosts of snow, falling faint

    as words while we try to find
Robert Johnson's muddy
    maybe grave. Beside Little Zion,

along the highwayside, this stone
    keeps its offerings—Bud & Louisiana
Hot Sauce—the ground giving

    way beneath our feet.
The blues always dance
    cheek to cheek with a church—

Booker's Place back
    in Greenwood still standing,
its long green bar

    beautiful, Friendship Church just
a holler away. Shotgun,
    shotgun, shotgun—

*

rows of colored
        houses, as if the same can
of bright stain might cover the sins

        of rotting wood, now
mostly tarpaper & graffiti
        holding McLaurin Street together—

RIP Boochie—the undead walk
        these streets seeking something
we take pictures of

        & soon flee. The hood
of a car yawns open
        in awe, men's heads

peer in its lion's mouth
        seeking their share. FOR SALE:
Squash & *Snap Beans.* The midden

        of oyster shells behind Lusco's—
the tiny O of a bullethole
        in Booker's plate glass window.

                    *

Even the Salvation
        Army Thrift Store
closed, bars over

                every door.
We're on our way again,
        away, along the Money

Road, past grand houses
        & porte cocheres set back
from the lane, across the bridge

        to find markers of what's
no more there—even the underpass
        bears a name. It's all

too grave—the fake
        sharecropper homes
of Tallahatchie Flats rented out

        along the road, staged bottle trees
chasing away nothing, the new outhouse
        whose crescent door foreign tourists

                        *

pay extra for. Cotton planted
        in strict rows
for show. A quiet

        snowglobe of pain
I want to shake.
        While the flakes fall

like ash we race
        the train to reach the place
Emmett Till last

        whistled or smiled
or did nothing.
        Money more

a crossroads
        than the crossroads be—
its gnarled tree—the Bryant Store

        facing the tracks, now turnt
the color of earth, tumbling down
        slow as the snow, white

                    *

& insistent as the woman
        who sent word
of that uppity boy, her men

        who yanked you out
your uncle's home
        into the yard, into oblivion—

into this store abutting
        the MONEY GIN CO.
whose sign, worn away,

            now reads UN
Or SIN, I swear—
        whose giant gin fans,

like those lashed & anchored
        to your beaten body,
still turn. Shot, dumped,

        dredged, your face not even
a mask—a marred,
        unspared, sightless stump—

                    *

all your mother insists
        we must see to know
What they did

        to my baby. The true
Tallahatchie twisting south,
        the Delta

Death's second cousin
        once removed. You down
for only the summer, to leave

        the stifling city where later
you will be waked,
        displayed, defiant,

a dark glass.
        There are things
that cannot be seen

        but must be. Buried
barely, this place
        no one can keep—

                        *

Yet how to kill
        a ghost? The fog
of our outdoor talk—

        we breathe,
we grieve, we drink
        our tidy drinks. I think

now winter will out—
        the snow bless
& kiss

        this cursed earth.
Or is it cussed? I don't
        yet know. Let the cold keep

still your bones.

IN A ROOM OF ONE THOUSAND BUDDHAS

Monica Sok

—ANGKOR NATIONAL MUSEUM, SIEM REAP

The water in my heart was falling. To my right
a row of Buddhas in meditation
sheltered by the Naga snake but this snake was real,
unlike the official snake in America who appointed
several other snakes to his cabinet.
The Naga protected the Buddha from rain,
spread its seven hoods to keep him dry.
And did I tell you it was raining all day?
I bought a poncho to ride around Siem Reap.
Rain during the dry season. Buddha calling on the Earth
for witness. Something water protectors
at Standing Rock are doing right now. Protecting water
because water is life. But a night of rubber bullets
and tear gas and water hoses, that is not life.
Today too, while eating breakfast noodles in my hotel
Neo-Nazis saluted the orange-skinned snake.
They were not calling on the Earth, their palms up
but facing down. Looking at the Buddha
I thought, he looks like me.
Some with broader shoulders, some from pre-Angkorian
and Angkorian times, some from this century,
four sitting back-to-back in a circle
each in different mudras. Sandstone. Wood. Stone.
Depending on what was available

or how kings chose to perpetuate who they worshipped.
Sitting on the coils of the Naga. Eyes closed.
Or looking down. Some looked scared. Calm.
Some with hands missing or cracked down the side.
Some looked starved. Their clothes shattered.
One, wooden, was defaced standing.
Except for a small curve of lip and one shut left eye.
There were others, smaller, as small as people.

SUPERIOR ALOESWOOD

Paul Muldoon

In memory of Leonard Cohen

I light a stick of Superior Aloeswood
from the box you gave me on South Tremaine
when last I visited. You'd conducted us through your new CD,
Professor Bob and myself tapping out a rhythm
on our cans of soda
while Nicodemus and Joseph of Arimathea
stayed back in the mix. Even as the aloeswood's musk-sweet
drifts through my kitchen I determine

how determinedly you refused to blend
a sorrow-base with a top note of solace.
Hard to make light of Bashar al-Assad turning his bombardiers
on his own citizenry (*grâce à* Putin),
while our vain, vindictive Pompadour
is pushing every button
on the console. During their break at the processing plant
the Mexicans are celebrating All Souls'

with *chilaquiles,* there being no circumstance so bland
a little extra salsa
won't kick it up. That August afternoon in Tinsel Town
we touched on how Europe's
right-wing nationalism is so in tune
with our own. The one note produced by the jaw harps

was more than enough for the Jews of Poland,
most of them conveyed from Silesia

to Auschwitz-Birkenau only after ponying up
for their own tickets.
Though we'd hoped to meet at the Blue Plate Oysterette
you'd been confined to barracks
on account of the side effects, I surmised, of steroids.
Not periwinkles, Nicodemus. *Periwigs!*
And though they went for $5 a pop
I used to favor a half-dozen Belons from the Damariscotta

over a dozen Wellfleets. Hard not to think of Pip,
the cabin boy of the *Pequod,*
forced to eat all that traif.
Hard not to think of him learning to flense
blubber from a whale like a turf-cutter cutting turf
on his smallholding. There was a little flourish on the violins
when you so graciously offered myself and Professor Bob
some cheddar or aged Gouda

and I happened to ask if you were a fan of Époisses—
the "King of Cheeses,"
according to Brillat-Savarin. I must have been in manic
mode when I'd have Murray's FedEx you a round
only hours after getting back to New York. A Cistercian monk
has been known to obsessively rinse the rind
in the pomace brandy that gives it such extra pizazz.
Why the electorate chooses

the likes of Ronald Bonzo and George W. Bozo
as Commander-in-Chief has already defied exegesis.
Hard not to think of Starbuck opening the waterproof match keg
and contriving to light a lamp of hope
while Tashtego, Daggoo, and Queequeg
despair of the vengeful Ahab.
When Nicodemus busies
himself treating the body of Jesus

"with a mixture of myrrh and aloes,
about an hundred pound weight,"
this "aloes" is our self-same aloeswood, beaten to a pulp
and thereafter prized
as an embalming agent from Beirut through Bologna to Bilbao.
It seems particularly appropriate that a priest
should also distill brandy from the lees
of wine. Not one iota

of aloeswood shall derive from the Aquilara tree
till it's threatened by a mold.
Only when a gold-orange
bloom of bacteria is allowed to seep
through a rind-washed cheese is its raunchy
essence revealed. Only when a sponge on a stalk of hyssop
is proffered him does Christ acknowledge the glitter
of the doubloon nailed to the mast is both amulet

against the whale and emblem of Burgundian caseiculture.
"Trouble is," you e-mailed

in October of your new favorite, Époisses,
"it's the only thing I want to eat."
Only when it's threatened does the Aquilara push
back with the fragrant gum that translates to *agar* or *oud*.
Egoless, aquiline, *égalitaire,*
you yourself had tried no less to emulate

the teachings of the abbot of Mount Baldy
than his famous locum,
Bernard of Clairvaux. I suspect Bernard had a hand
in the development of the Meursault
Jefferson would come to love. Hard to reconcile the whale hunt
with the thirteen attributes of Divine Mercy
now that Ahab pilots the pilot
away from our ninth and final gam

and, having tempered his barb in the blood
of Queequeg, Tashtego, and Daggoo, offers his final *l'chaim*
while urging us to stand firm. A chasuble
is a version of a "little house." A kind of poncho.
It was no time after Jezebel
had married Ahab that she took it upon herself to banish
the prophets of Israel and trade them for the polity
of Baal. In the matter of leukemia,

of course, it comes down to the bone marrow
producing freak blood cells. Let's not forget how the brazen
serpent becomes a false idol
to which the Israelites cry Hallelujah

and make their own offerings of incense. One jot or one tittle
shall in no way pass from the law
till Abraham sacrifices Ishmael on Mount Moriah.
The incense-smoke sends up its orison

over Mounts Moriah and Meru.
That August afternoon our *tour d'horizon*
included not only the Tower of Wrong
being built by Trump
from the promises on which he'll shortly renege
but the life-size diorama
of a grove of trees. Those same trees producing myrrh
only when they're wounded. Just as the resin

in a stick of Superior Aloeswood
is produced only as an immune response
to an all-out attack. It's not only Bashar al-Assad
dropping barrel-bombs on his people that threatens the core
of our humanity. In the meantime, the sweat
from a round of Époisses raises its own Kyrie
through the kitchen to mingle with the funky incense-soot.
Not harps, Nicodemus. Not harps. *Harpoons!*

EVERY DAY   *Robin Coste Lewis*

After Jean Rhys & Charlotte Brontë

I was born in the attic
because Mother claimed
brown the more honest name
for *beige.* They hit her—

the doctor, the priest, her
mother. She sat alone
all day, spitting her teeth
out like pomegranate.

There is this large putrid jar
beneath our bed. I came
after she climbed out
too often with the yard man

to lay cane. Now our days
will be out of doors, instead
of inside them; our future will lie
with petals, caterpillars, well-dressed

moss, hypnotic snails, clapping
orange frogs that know to climb
which tree for the ripest alligator
pear. Every ocean has known us,

Mother says, no shore is insignificant.
For every ship, still, the smallest sea
can be too wide. The world sits on the edge
of God's razor, she says. And every day—

every day—He shaves
His fat face.

NOW

Frederick Seidel

For Robert Silvers

And you could say we've been living in clover
From Walt Whitman to Barack Obama.
Now a dictatorship of vicious spineless slimes
We the people voted in has taken over.
Once we'd abolished slavery, we lived in clover,
From sea to shining sea, even in terrible times.
It's over.

Look how the sunlight enters the bedroom and my dream.
Look how the radio alarm attacks me with an ax.
The plane I have to catch departs at eight from JFK.
Unbuckled and at cruising altitude, we'll excrete a white contrail.
I have to be there two hours before
We do. How beautiful the sky when you're below.
The Russian ambassador to Turkey was gunned down

Giving a friendship speech at an art gallery in Ankara
By a Turkish Islamic zealot
Pointing one finger upward and saying God is great.
Do not forget Aleppo! Do not forget Syria! he shouts,
Referring to the horror and the thousands wretchedly dead,
The little children, from Russian aerial bombing.
Russia is red and red the blood the ambassador bled.

The body on the floor
Is the late ambassa door.
You step over him to your study window holding a loaded gun
To your head and jump
Out to your death into the arms of Donald Trump.
Pigeons have painted the ledge outside the window white.
Now the day is over and it is time to say good night.

I hear the pillow hissing *auf wiedersehen.*
I stumble out of bed and start sleepwalking.
WWW, White Western World, stand on your feet to greet,
    still asleep,
The arrival of the bride made of daylight all dressed in white.
Outbursts of pigeons explode white
As light in whorls of flight in the wonderful sunlight,
Then settle on cooing ledges and shit white.

I'm trumpeting the most dazzling imitation
Diamond ring you'll ever see,
Set by the expat genius jeweler JAR in Paris,
Whom nothing ostentatious can embarrass,
To celebrate the catastrophe of America, the American catastrophe.
The only possession of mine
God will want to grab

Is on my pinkie
When I'm laid out naked on the slab,
And here comes God—who's of course a she—
Who removes the ring,
And slides my corpse
For cremation
Into her big hot thing.

There was a very rich
Lady who lived on Liberty Island,
Who lied to herself and the world like Donald Trump.
Her druggy daughter, her only child,
Whose memory she liked to weep over and about whom she lied,
Had lived and died years before, and apparently the mother
Had behaved horribly when the daughter badly needed her.

The woman was arrogant.
People loved her.
Her life was luxurious. People like that.
There was an old
Woman who lived in a shoe.
Her fantasy was that she and her daughter
Had been fantastic together.

A person who smokes cigarettes these days,
Albeit only secretly,
A woman who smokes but hides it so no one sees,
And is careful about how she smells, no stink, no stain, no pain,
Now it begins to rain
In her lungs, these days when you're not permitted to smoke
    anywhere inside
A public place, even if she's elegant, is ashamed.

Give the poor bitch a break.
Be kind to poor inhuman us.
Aren't we all a bit like her and at least a little fake?
And wasn't America often quite generous?
In fact, my understanding is the Western heart is leaking pus
And the Western brain is near the end.
The Prophet Muhammad and his evil double have started to blend.

The President of the United States proclaims America First.
He doesn't know Mecca from Milan.
There's been a terrorist attack in Berlin.
Also, the leader of North Korea
Has ordered a new diet for border guards
That has given them diarrhea.
I repeatedly shot an innocent unarmed black man in the back
    who was fleeing

Into a park full of broad daylight. Good morning.
If you're a senior citizen, you won't really live long
Enough to know
The river of refugees has reversed its course,
Flowing the wrong way now on account of shock
And aftershocks and so many fools saying
Have a good day.

The United States of America, its ribs gauntly sticking out,
Tries to drink from a watering hole, all fifty states try,
Bulls mooing like cows, Gestapo everywhere,
But there's no water,
And this is not just in Flint, Michigan.
Girls and boys, a world you never knew is over.
I was writing a poem the other day that said so.

It said we've been living in clover
From Walt Whitman to Barack Obama.
Once we'd abolished slavery, we lived in clover
From sea to shining sea, even in terrible times.
Now a dictatorship of spineless vicious slimes
We the people voted into power has taken over
And it's over.

ONE WORLD TRADE   *Danielle Chapman*

The rack of whale ribs flung:

gargantuan iron
toothpicks and gauze

optimism swaddling the site.

Then the warp-angled platinum
tower rising to a height

so defiant it conjures a comic book
Apocalypse, clouds row-

ing swiftly past as if all
of us below were riding it; while

atop the awning, a Sudanese
worker turns the O

in WORLD to polish it.

THIS BEAUTIFUL BUBBLE   *Vincent Katz*

I love this bubble,
Everyone takes the subway, and you can look up,
And look at all the people, and each one is different,
And they *look* different, and each one has a story, and
    suddenly,
You are awake and want to know each story, only you can't,
Don't have time, they don't, don't want to maybe.

But some you do, you glean, you approximate yourself to
    something of them,
Like the beautiful, chestnut-skinned woman, who, leaning,
Listened to the announcer before getting in, and, confused,
    because the 2 was called a 5,
Asked advice, and three people responded,
Explaining in their different ways, some of them silent,
Eyes met with approval, warmth only subway-known,
Among equals, fellow travelers, denizens;

She sat and smiled, and looking at an infant,
Smiled more, her hair was a flag of self-joy too,
She was real, at ease among people.
The rule is: to speak.
Make contact, and you will find people more beautiful than
    you thought.

But back to our bubble. It is everywhere around us.
Everywhere, walking in the city, you are seeing people,

All different kinds, shapes, sizes, the best education
You can give a child is to bring them up inside this
Beautiful bubble. I complain, but I'll never leave.
I feed off the looks, the stories, the hungering here.

I'm aware, we're all aware, what goes on outside the bubble.
We're not stupid. We just thought people outside the bubble
    wanted the same thing:
To live as variously as possible.
Or, put another way: I am the least difficult of men.
All I want is boundless love.

It took us sixty years or so to understand
What the word "boundless" meant.
Now we know. And we'll never forget.

AFTER THE END

Andrea Cohen

Listen, there were other
ends, other reckonings.

There were other one-
size boots, one kick

fits all. There were
other dark days no

night could mirror.
Hear me out—

if someone
above the rubble can.

ASSEMBLY   *Christian Wiman*

It may be Lord our voice is suited now
only for irony, onslaught, and the minor hierarchies of rage.

It may be that only the crudest, cruelest transformations
    touch us,
gauzewalkers in the hallways of a burn ward.

I remember a blind man miraculous for the sounds of his
    mouth,
every bird rehearsed and released for the children to cheer.

Where is he now, in what icy facility or sunlit square,
blackout shades and a brambled mouth, singing extinctions?

SONG OF OURSELVES (CENTO) *Amit Majmudar*

Now that Captain America is dead
and no one saves anyone
                              to whom do you
pray?

            That poem your father
wrote you was a fucking living weapon.
Many turn to magic for protection.

I sing of arms
given to me by an Indian woman,
of bullets we laughed at
in the gray hour before dawn—
our national wound
                              the O
in WORLD.

To live as variously as possible
                              I would die
for my country
if that included
the Mexicans celebrating All Souls'
in the changed air
bluer than bruises,
that scent of wet barricades,
the river of refugees

too late for hope
further and further cut off from woods and river.

Charlatan, huckster, grifter,
fraud:
Some people love death so much they want to give it to everyone.
I wasn't made by their god.

For my task is to praise all I don't understand:
        the mysteries of building houses in water,
        how the mountain
        became a spear,
        Eve's freckles,
        blue parakeets
        homeless on the ocean. . . .

There was violence, and it did and didn't touch us
sunk in a lake.
               We (forgive us)
almost all
lived happily during the war.
Let them not say: we did not see it.

A night of rubber bullets
and tear gas.
His fat face
on my screen.

What the fuck are you crying for?

Fight and make music
after the markets crash
                here (*here!*)
like all the mobs in storybooks.

Set that on fire.

A certain beauty in the duty of it:
The pain in which we trust.
           Knuckle your eyes
in disbelief.
Peer in its lion's mouth.

Listen, there were other
ends, other reckonings—
blackout shades and a brambled mouth, singing extinctions.

Volunteer,
foreigner,
friend,

what on Earth are we?

                America   America   America

ACKNOWLEDGMENTS

Thank you to the journals, magazines, blogs, and other outlets in which many of these poems first appeared, and to Knopf's fellow book publishers, large and small, who participate in the important work of publishing poetry.

Ellen Bass's "Jubilate Homo" appeared in *Narrative.*

David Breskin's "Mountebank" appeared in *7-Elevens,* the daily blog of his "Elective Poems," and is forthcoming in the collection *Campaign* (MadHat Press and Audible Studios).

Lucie Brock-Broido's "The American Security Against Foreign Enemies Act" appeared in *The New Yorker.*

Andrea Cohen's "After the End" appeared in *Construction.*

Eduardo C. Corral's "Border Patrol Agent" appeared in *The New Republic.*

Chard deNiord's "The Beavers" appeared on *Poetry Daily.*

Forrest Gander's "The Sounding" is forthcoming in *Resist Much/ Obey Little* (Spuyten Duyvil, 2017).

Bob Hicok's "We've come a long way toward getting nowhere" appeared in *Rise Up Review.*

Jane Hirshfield's "Let Them Not Say" appeared on January 20, 2017 (inauguration day), in Poets.org's "Poem-a-Day" series.

Richie Hofmann's "Children of the Sun" appeared in *Prodigal.*

Fady Joudah's "National Park" appeared on *Poetry Now* and is forthcoming in *Footnotes in the Order of Disappearance* (Milkweed Editions, 2018).

Ilya Kaminsky's "We Lived Happily During the War" appeared in *The American Poetry Review.*

Vincent Katz's "This Beautiful Bubble" is forthcoming in *Resist Much/Obey Little* (Spuyten Duyvil, 2017).

Richard Kenney's "Civics One: Our Democracy" appeared in *Poetry Northwest.*

Joanna Klink's "New Year" appeared in Poets.org's "Poem-a-Day" series.

Dana Levin's "'You Will Never Get Death / Out of Your System'" appeared, in a different form and under the title "Fortune Cookie," as part of the Poetry Society of America's "In Their Own Words" series.

Robin Coste Lewis's "Every Day" appeared in *T Magazine*.

Ada Limón's "Killing Methods" appeared on the blog "What Rough Beast."

Joshua Mehigan's "The Source" appeared in *The Hopkins Review*.

Tomás Q. Morín's "112th Congress Blues" appeared in *The American Poetry Review*.

Paul Muldoon's "Superior Aloeswood" appeared in *The New York Review of Books*.

Carol Muske-Dukes's "Some Say" is forthcoming, in slightly different form, in *Bullets into Bells,* a Beacon Press anthology about gun violence.

Robert Pinsky's "Exile and Lightning," commissioned as an inaugural poem for the January 15, 2017, PEN/Writers Resist event in New York, appeared online on CNN's Opinion page.

Frederick Seidel's "Now" appeared on the *Paris Review* blog, "The Daily."

Solmaz Sharif's "Social Skills Training" appeared on Buzzfeed.com.

Maggie Smith's "Good Bones" appeared in *Waxwing* and is forthcoming in *Weep Up* (Tupelo Press, 2017).

"Aegean Blues," from **A. E. Stallings's** "Refugee Fugue," appeared in *The Raintown Review,* and was set to music by the Switzerland-based band Human Shields; "Appendix A" appeared in the web zine *Partisan*.

Cody Walker's "Sitting on a Sofa in a 1925 Bungalow in Ann Arbor, Michigan" appeared on Terrain.org and in the chapbook *The Trumpiad* (Waywiser Press).

Christian Wiman's "Assembly" appeared in *The Yale ISM Review*.

David Yezzi's "Plague" appeared in *Smartish Pace*.

Kevin Young's "Money Road" appeared in *The New Yorker* and is forthcoming in *Brown* (Knopf, 2018) and *The Best American Poetry 2017*.

CONTRIBUTORS

James Arthur lives in Baltimore, where he teaches in the Writing Seminars at Johns Hopkins University. His first book, *Charms Against Lightning,* was published in 2012 by Copper Canyon Press.

Ellen Bass's most recent book is *Like a Beggar* and her poems appear frequently in *The New Yorker* and *The American Poetry Review.* A chancellor of the Academy of American Poets, she teaches in Pacific University's MFA program.

David Breskin, a recovering journalist, is a poet, record producer, and culture worker who lives in San Francisco.

Lucie Brock-Broido's most recent book is *Stay, Illusion* (Knopf, 2013). She is the director of poetry in the School of the Arts at Columbia University and lives in Cambridge, Massachusetts, and New York City.

Jericho Brown is a Guggenheim Fellow whose poems have appeared in *The New York Times* and *The New Yorker.* His most recent book is *The New Testament* (Copper Canyon Press, 2014).

Danielle Chapman's poetry collection, *Delinquent Palaces,* was published by Northwestern University Press in 2015. She teaches creative writing at Yale.

Andrea Cohen's most recent poetry collection is *Unfathoming;* she directs the Blacksmith House Poetry Series in Cambridge, Massachusetts, and the Writers House at Merrimack College.

Eduardo C. Corral's first book, *Slow Lightning,* won the Yale Series of Younger Poets competition.

Erica Dawson is the author of two collections of poetry: *Big-Eyed Afraid* and *The Small Blades Hurt.* She is the director of the University of Tampa's Low-Residency MFA program.

Chard deNiord is the Poet Laureate of Vermont and author of six books of poetry, most recently *Interstate* and *The Double Truth,* both from the University of Pittsburgh Press. He is a professor of English and creative writing at Providence College.

Michael Dickman was born and raised in the Pacific Northwest.

Alex Dimitrov is the author of two books of poems, *Together and by Ourselves* (Copper Canyon Press, 2017) and *Begging for It* (Four Way Books, 2013). He lives in New York City.

Forrest Gander's most recent books are *Alice, Iris, Red Horse: Selected Poems of Gozo Yoshimasu* and *Then Come Back: The Lost Neruda Poems*.

Rebecca Hazelton is the author of *Fair Copy* (Ohio State University Press), and *Vow* (Cleveland State University Press). Her poems have been published in *Poetry, The New Yorker*, and *The Best American Poetry 2013*.

Juan Felipe Herrera, a multi-genre poet, has produced children's books, middle-grade, YA novels, and art. He was Poet Laureate of the United States from 2015 to 2017; he directs the Laureate Lab at California State University, Fresno.

Bob Hicok's most recent book is *Sex & Love &* (Copper Canyon Press, 2016).

Jane Hirshfield's most recent books are *The Beauty: Poems* and *Ten Windows: How Great Poems Transform the World*. She is a current chancellor of the Academy of American Poets.

Richie Hofmann's debut collection of poems is *Second Empire* (Alice James Books, 2015).

Fady Joudah's poetry and poetry in translation have earned national and international awards, including a Yale Series of Younger Poets competition and the Griffin International Poetry Prize.

Ilya Kaminsky was born in Ukraine and currently lives in California. He is the author of *Dancing in Odessa* (Tupelo Press, 2004) and coeditor of *The Ecco Anthology of International Poetry* (Ecco/HarperCollins, 2010).

Vincent Katz is the author of the poetry collections *Southness* and *Swimming Home*. He lives in New York and teaches at the Yale University School of Art.

Richard Kenney's last book was *The One-Strand River* (Knopf, 2008). He teaches at the University of Washington and lives with his family on the Olympic Peninsula.

Joanna Klink is the author of four books of poetry, most recently *Excerpts from a Secret Prophecy* (Penguin, 2015). She teaches in the Creative Writing Program at the University of Montana.

Deborah Landau is the author of three books of poetry, most recently *The Uses of the Body*. She is the recipient of a 2016 Guggenheim Fellowship and directs the Creative Writing Program at New York University.

Dana Levin is the author of four books of poetry, most recently *Banana Palace* (Copper Canyon Press, 2016). She serves as distinguished writer in residence at Maryville University in Saint Louis.

Robin Coste Lewis is the author of *Voyage of the Sable Venus.*

Ada Limón is the author of four books of poetry, including *Bright Dead Things,* which was named a finalist for the National Book Award, the National Book Critics Circle Award, and the Kingsley Tufts Poetry Award.

Dave Lucas is the author of *Weather,* which received the 2012 Ohioana Book Award for Poetry. He lives in Cleveland.

Amit Majmudar's next volume, forthcoming from Knopf in 2018, is a verse translation from the Sanskrit of the Bhagavad Gita, entitled *Godsong.*

Joshua Mehigan has received fellowships from the NEA and the Guggenheim Foundation. His second book, *Accepting the Disaster,* was published in 2014 by Farrar, Straus and Giroux.

Tomás Q. Morín is the author of *Patient Zero* and *A Larger Country,* and the translator of Pablo Neruda's *The Heights of Macchu Picchu.*

Paul Muldoon is Howard G. B Clark University Professor of the Humanities at Princeton. His most recent book is *Selected Poems 1968–2014,* published by Farrar, Straus and Giroux in 2016.

Carol Muske-Dukes's ninth book of poems, *Blue Rose,* is forthcoming (Penguin Poets Series, 2018). She is a former Poet Laureate of California and a professor at the University of Southern California.

Eileen Myles has published twenty books including the upcoming *Afterglow* (a dog memoir) and most recently *I Must Be Living Twice: New and Selected Poems* and a reissue of their novel *Chelsea Girls.* They live in Marfa, Texas, and New York.

D. Nurkse is the author of eleven poetry collections, including the forthcoming *Love in the Last Days;* he has also served on the board of Amnesty International USA and written on human rights issues.

Sharon Olds, winner of the Pulitzer Prize for *Stag's Leap,* is most recently the author of *Odes* and teaches in the graduate program in creative writing at NYU.

Rowan Ricardo Phillips's most recent book is *Heaven* (Farrar, Straus and Giroux, 2015). He lives in New York City and Barcelona.

Robert Pinsky's most recent book of poems is *At the Foundling*

Hospital. He founded the Favorite Poem Project, with videos at www.favoritepoem.org.

Kay Ryan's most recent book is *Erratic Facts.*

Frederick Seidel lives in New York City.

Solmaz Sharif is the author of *Look* (Graywolf Press, 2016), a finalist for the National Book Award, and is currently a lecturer at Stanford University.

Maggie Smith is the author of *Weep Up* (Tupelo Press, September 2017), *The Well Speaks of Its Own Poison, Lamp of the Body,* and three prizewinning chapbooks.

Monica Sok is a Khmer poet from Lancaster, Pennsylvania, and the author of *Year Zero,* winner of a Chapbook Fellowship from Poetry Society of America.

David St. John's most recent collection is *The Last Troubadour: New and Selected Poems* (Ecco/HarperCollins, 2017). He lives in Venice Beach and is chair of English at the University of Southern California.

A. E. Stallings is an American poet and translator who has lived in Athens since 1999; she has been active volunteering in Athens with the refugee crisis in Greece since November 2015.

Cody Walker is the author of *The Self-Styled No-Child* (Waywiser, 2016) and *Shuffle and Breakdown* (Waywiser, 2008). He teaches at the University of Michigan.

Christian Wiman's most recent book is *Hammer Is the Prayer: Selected Poems.*

David Yezzi's most recent books of poems are *Birds of the Air* (2013) and, forthcoming in 2018, *Black Sea,* both from Carnegie Mellon.

Dean Young's most recent book is *Shock by Shock* (Copper Canyon Press, 2015).

Kevin Young is the director of the Schomburg Center for Research in Black Culture and the poetry editor of *The New Yorker.* His most recent books are *Blue Laws: Selected and Uncollected Poems, 1995–2015* and *Bunk,* a nonfiction account of the rise of hoaxes and fake news in American life.